CHOOSE YOUR OWN ADVEN

Kids Love

Choose Your O

"Thank you for making these books for kids.
I bet kids that haven't read it yet would love it.
All I can say is that I love your books and I
bet other kids would love them too."
Bella Foster, age 8

"These books are really cool. When I get to the
end of the page, it makes me want to keep going to
find out what is going to happen to me. I get to make
my own choices of what I WANT to happen next."
Bionca Samuel, age 10

"This book was good. I like that I got
to pick how the story went."
Lily Von Trapp, age 7

"I like how you can make up the story,
but it also tells you a story."
Liam Stewart, age 8

"I like to follow the princess and wonder
what is going to happen next."
Lilly Boyd, age 7

Thanks to Erin Falligant for all her writing help.

Illustrated by: Vladimir Semionov
Book design: Stacey Boyd, Big Eyedea Visual Design
For information regarding permission, write to:

CHOOSECO
P.O. Box 46
Waitsfield, Vermont 05673
www.cyoa.com

A DRAGONLARK BOOK

ISBN: 1-937133-54-0
EAN: 978-1-937133-54-2

Published simultaneously in the United States and Canada

Printed in the United States.

10 9 8 7 6 5 4 3 2 1

CHOOSE YOUR OWN ADVENTURE®

Princess Perri and the Second Summer

BY SHANNON GILLIGAN

A DRAGONLARK BOOK

For Melissa Bounty, with enormous gratitude and affection!

READ THIS FIRST!!!

WATCH OUT!
THIS BOOK IS DIFFERENT
from every book you've ever read.

Do not read this book from the first page
through to the last page.
Instead, start on page 1 and read until you
come to your first choice. Then turn to the
page shown and see what happens.

When you come to the end of a story,
you can go back and start again.
Every choice leads to a new adventure.

Good luck!

You race along the wooded path, following the sign toward the cabin named Indian Pipe. You've been waiting all year for your second summer at Princess Island. The first day at camp is finally here.

When you reach your cabin, the screen door flings open.

"Perri!" your best friend Princess Caroline of Ludmilia cries, bounding onto the porch.

"Caroline! We're cabinmates?" you squeal, giving her a hug.

"Yes!" your good friend nods happily.

Bizzy, Marchioness of Maximilia, one of your cabinmates from first year, sticks her head out the door next.

"So am I," Bizzy says with a grin.

"What a great cabin! Who's our fourth?" you ask, stepping inside the cabin.

Caroline and Bizzy exchange a funny look.

Turn to page 3.

A red-haired girl steps out of the shadows. You would recognize that sour face anywhere.

"Me," your second cousin Lady Millicent Smythe says. "I'm the fourth cabinmate, Peregrine."

"Millicent!" you exclaim. "I…um…I wasn't sure you were coming back."

"I didn't want to. Mother insisted," your cousin replies. "Since we're of higher rank, I thought you and I should share a bunk."

You blush at Millicent's rude comment about your friends. She's not even correct. Caroline is a Princess Regent and will rule Ludmilia when she turns eighteen. But there's no use arguing with Millicent.

"Actually," you say quickly, "I was hoping to bunk with Caroline."

Millicent's cheeks flush red, as if she's about to throw a fit.

Turn to the next page.

4

"I'll share your bunk, Millie," Bizzy offers. "You can have the top."

Millicent narrows her eyes. "My name is Millicent. Nicknames aren't very royal."

Bizzy grins and rolls her eyes so only you and Caroline can see. Her real name is Elizabeth, but "Bizzy" suits her. And she just saved you by swapping beds. You owe her one!

"Oh my gosh," Caroline says, looking at her watch. "Welcome lunch starts in three minutes. We better hurry." Caroline takes off, and the three of you follow.

You run past the cabins named Sheep Laurel and Trillium on your way to the Main Lodge. There are thirty-six cabins in all at Princess Island. Each one is named for a wildflower. Every cabin has four campers and one junior counselor.

Go on to the next page.

You reach the Main Lodge and dash up the front steps just as the final gong rings. Once inside, you all stop to look at the new, large display case.

"Wow," Caroline says, "the Cabin Cup is as beautiful as I remember."

The big silver trophy gleams quietly in the center of the display. It's awarded to the cabin with the highest score in the annual Princess Playoffs. The Cup is at least two feet tall, covered with vines and leaves, and weighs more than ten pounds!

"You know it's not the original Cabin Cup," Bizzy whispers.

"It isn't?" you ask.

You notice Millicent has walked ahead into the dining room. You and Caroline lean in.

Turn to page 7.

"My mom says the old one was even more beautiful," Bizzy explains. "And solid gold! It was stolen one summer and never found."

"Look," Caroline says. "Here it is!" She points to an old photo of proud campers on horseback, holding an ornate golden cup.

"Do they have any idea who did it?" you ask.

Bizzy lowers her voice. "They say it was stolen by the boys on Prince Island over thirty years ago. Reportedly it's buried somewhere here on the island. It was supposed to be a prank."

That figures, you think. Your brother, Harold, is at camp on Prince Island, and this sounds like something he and his dumb friends would do.

They are starting to sing the camp song. Your talk is cut short as you rush to join the others at your table for the welcome lunch. It's exciting to see all your old friends and meet some new ones. Everyone is having a good time except Millicent.

Turn to page 13.

The three of you work together. Caroline is using a stick to loosen the soil. Even Harold starts to scrape the dirt back with his foot. It's getting too dark to see well. Whatever it is, it's wrapped in an old sheet.

Finally, you pull it free. Carefully, you unwrap the sheet. The famous lost Princess Island Cabin Cup gleams in the fading light.

"We did it!" you cheer. You actually give Harold a hug. You couldn't have found the Cup without his map.

You and Caroline are so excited. "Thanks to Arts and Crafts class, we solved the mystery." At first that flower crafts class seemed too princess-like for a princess like you.

But you never know which princess skills are going to come in handy—or when!

"I think we might even win the Playoffs!" Caroline exclaims. "Wait till Mrs. Wiggins finds out."

The End

"Look what I found under my pillow," you say, showing the note to Bizzy and Millicent.

Bizzy's eyes grow narrow, and she leans in and whispers, "You should steer clear of the burial ground. Countess Rosaline Fox said that anyone who sets foot there suffers an ill fate. There's a curse to keep people away."

A curse? You want to ask more, but some campers from the Trillium cabin show up with a box of homemade fudge, and they're sharing.

That night, you have trouble falling asleep. You are thinking of turning on your flashlight when you hear the creak of the cabin door.

Who is that?! You roll over just as Bizzy tiptoes out.

"Where's she going?" Caroline whispers.

"I don't know," you say. "But let's go find out."

You both slide into your sandals and sneak out the door, careful not to wake Millicent.

Turn to the next page.

You spot Bizzy disappearing down the path toward the beach. You wait at the edge of the clearing and watch her sneak into the boathouse. A few seconds later, Bizzy emerges paddling a small canoe. She heads east.

"Where's she going?" Caroline whispers. "There's nothing in that direction."

"Except the burial ground," you reply.

"What do we do?" asks Caroline.

"We go after her," you answer.

"We can't canoe at night! It's dangerous! I don't even have my solo boating permission yet," she replies.

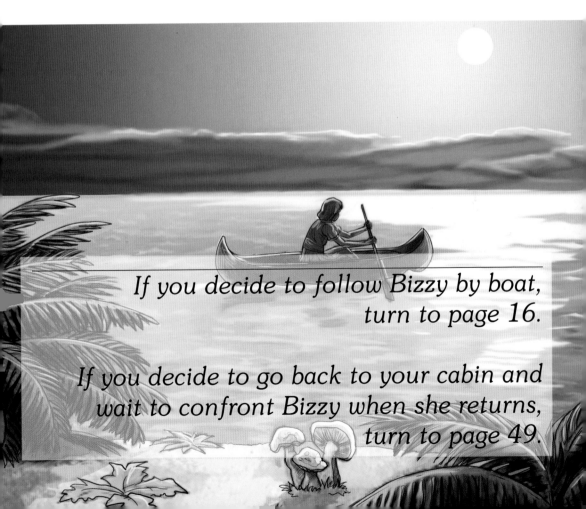

If you decide to follow Bizzy by boat, turn to page 16.

If you decide to go back to your cabin and wait to confront Bizzy when she returns, turn to page 49.

"We can try to include you more, Millicent," you say.

"Maybe we can watch your play rehearsal!" suggests Caroline. "You're a good actress. You sure gave us the willies tonight."

"Lady Millie gave you the willies?" jokes Bizzy. She clamps her hand over her mouth. "Sorry."

But Millicent isn't mad about the nickname. She actually laughs.

You didn't solve the mystery of the strange note. But you might have turned a cousin into a friend.

The End

After lunch, there's free time while new campers take the required swim test. Back at Indian Pipe, you flop onto your bed to write a letter to your mom. She camped here as a girl. Now she's Queen. Maybe she knows something about the missing Cabin Cup!

Just as you finish writing, something catches your eye—a pink note tucked beneath your pillow. It reads:

MEET ME AT THE BURIAL GROUND AT 9:00 TONIGHT.

DON'T FORGET TO BRING THE MAP!

Turn to the next page.

You read the note twice. No one is supposed to be out after dark. And the burial ground on the other side of the island is off limits—everyone knows that!

"Who do you think wrote this?" you ask Caroline, showing her the note.

She examines it closely. Her eyes open wide. "Should we ask Bizzy or Millicent?"

If you share the strange note with Bizzy and Millicent, turn to page 9.

If you share the strange note with Bizzy and Millicent, turn to page 9.

If you decide to keep the note a secret, turn to page 20.

"Let's follow Bizzy in a rowboat," you say. "That'll be safer."

You run to the boathouse, put on your life vests, and hop in. You row as quickly as you can. Soon you see lights flickering ahead.

Is it Bizzy?

Are they coming from Witch's Hat rock?

Or from Prince Island?

A sudden gust of wind rocks the boat. Caroline grips the sides and says, "It's going to storm. We should go back. We don't even know if that's Bizzy shining those lights!"

If you call out to Bizzy, go to page 27.

If you follow the lights, go to page 56.

Soon you can touch bottom with your feet.
You walk the rest of the way to shore.
"Where are we?" Caroline sputters.

Turn to page 81.

Bizzy and Millicent suddenly burst into the cabin. Millicent is telling Bizzy a story about everything she's done this summer before camp. You quickly slide the note back under your pillow.

"What are you two up to?" asks Bizzy.

"Nothing!" you and Caroline say at the exact same time.

Millicent narrows her eyes like she suspects something. But she says nothing.

"The advanced swim test starts soon," Bizzy announces. "I'm going to try for it. Are you?"

Go on to the next page.

The advanced swimmer's badge allows you to do most water sports solo.

"I'm going to try," you say, hopping up.

"Me too," Caroline says.

"I have no intention of taking the advanced swim test, now or ever," Millicent announces. "Kayaking is not ladylike. I'm going to read a book."

You and Caroline just smile at your silly cousin. Millicent's attitude is probably going to hurt your chances for the Cabin Cup. But there is not much you can do.

You make your way down to the beach where the swim tests take place. Your year of swimming lessons has paid off. You qualify for Experienced Swimmer. Caroline does not, however.

"Don't worry, you can try again in two weeks," a counselor tells her. She nods, but you can tell she's disappointed.

Turn to the next page.

That night at the dinner table, you whisper to Caroline, "I have to know what's happening at the burial ground. Will you come with me?"

She shivers. "What if we run into the ghost of Lady Violet Grimm?"

All Princess Island campers love stories about the lady in white who haunts the island.

You and Caroline saw her last year. You learned she was searching for her long lost love.

"She's just a ghost right?" you say. "And ghosts can only scare you. They can't really hurt you. Plus, my nanny, Miss York, says we should face our fears head-on."

Caroline hesitates. "Okay, I'll come," she finally says. What a good friend!

Turn to the next page.

While Millicent is snoring, you and Caroline tiptoe out of the cabin.

You walk the dirt path in the moonlight. When you reach the oldest, thickest part of the forest, Caroline stops. "Do we have to go through *that* part of the woods?" she asks.

"It's the quickest way," you say, reaching for her hand.

The forest *is* dark. You can barely *see* the path ahead. You thought the full moon would be enough. You should have brought flashlights. As the wind picks up, the leaves whisper. Then you hear a low, eerie howl coming from nearby.

Caroline sucks in her breath. "What's that?"

"Just the wind," you say quickly. "I think it might storm later." But the hairs stand up on your arms. *Maybe this wasn't such a great idea*, you think.

Turn to page 30.

You call out Bizzy's name. Your voice echoes off the water.

There's a moment of silence. It sounds like people talking. Someone laughs.

Who is it? you wonder. You and Caroline continue to row. A bank of mist appears. The voices are coming from inside the mist. Is it Bizzy?

It suddenly becomes easier to row, as if someone else is pulling the oars.

"Just one kiss, Violet," a man's voice says.

"Do you love me?" a young woman asks. "You can kiss me if you love me."

"I love you more than the moon and the stars," the young man answers. "I love you more than life itself."

Suddenly a ghostly couple in a ghostly canoe appears. It's Lady Violet, the Princess Island ghost, and her secret love, Mathew!

Caroline gasps.

Turn to page 31.

You decide to go back to check on Millicent. She wasn't fibbing this time. The ghost of Lady Violet Grimm towers over her, glowing white and angry. "How dare you mock me!" she shouts, her hands on her hips.

Millicent covers her face and starts to cry. You feel sorry for your cousin. So sorry that you don't even feel scared—you feel brave.

"We'll take her away, Lady Violet. We'll make sure she doesn't bother you anymore."

The ghost stares into your eyes, as if she can see right through you. "Get that nasty girl out of my sight!"she yells.

"Come with me!" you say to Millicent. "Now!"

Millicent whimpers as she stumbles after you and Caroline. You glance over your shoulder. Lady Violet is still watching you and she starts to float in your direction. You turn back and run faster.

Turn to page 84.

Caroline walks close behind. As you round a bend in the trail, you see a soft lavender glow, low to the ground. Seeing it makes your stomach cold.

"It's the ghost!" Caroline cries. "Run!"

"Wait! Are you sure?" you say, peering ahead.

If you stay and convince Caroline to keep going, turn to page 32.

If you decide to head back to Indian Pipe, turn to page 57.

"What was that?" Violet says. She twists around and stares right at you. She cannot be more then ten feet away.

But she looks right through you.

"We had better return," Lady Violet says.

"Only because after tomorrow we'll be together forever," Mathew answers.

He begins to paddle back toward Princess Island. Your rowboat seems to be magically tethered to the two of them.

You watch in amazement as Mathew paddles Lady Violet to shore, helps her from the boat, and kisses her goodbye. He paddles off into the mist. Lady Violet waves until he disappears.

A terrible feeling of sadness comes over you both.

"This must be the last time they saw each other," Caroline says.

Turn to page 43.

"Wait! I don't think it's a ghost," you say. "Let's see what it is. I'll go first."

As you tiptoe along the trail, your heart thuds in your ears. But as you get close, you realize the source of the eerie glow. It's a cluster of plants growing beside a beech tree. The stems and bell-shaped flowers are ghostly white. They glow strongly enough to cast a light on the ferns and moss around them.

"Wow. Creepy," Caroline whispers. "Let's keep going!"

You hurry past the white flowers. When the trees thin out, you breathe a sigh of relief. Then you smack into a two-foot-tall boulder.

"Perri!" gasps Caroline in an urgent voice. "Don't move!"

You are afraid to look around. "Why?" you say.

Turn to the next page.

"It's a grave!" Caroline says to you.

The tombstone is all by itself. You look around. It sits in a pretty part of the forest, with willow and beech trees planted nearby.

The name on the gravestone is familiar: GRIMM.

"Oh my goodness. Do you think it belongs to Lady Violet Grimm?!" says Caroline, her voice rising.

A shiver runs down your spine.

Then you both hear a strange scraping noise. You freeze.

"Someone's digging another grave!" you whisper. Caroline is as pale as a ghost herself.

"There!" you say pointing. You see a girl with a shovel. You duck down behind the gravestone, pulling Caroline with you.

The gravedigger turns around. It's Bizzy's friend Sam!

Relief floods your chest. You hurry forward. She looks confused to see you.

Turn to page 37.

"Where's Bizzy?" Sam asks. "Didn't she get the note I left?"

It takes you a second to put it together. "No!" you laugh. "I got the note instead. Bizzy and I swapped beds. What are you doing out here?"

Sam sighs and leans on her shovel.

"I'm looking for the missing Cabin Cup. Bizzy and I found a map that showed the Cup buried here, by a tree. But I can't find it!" Sam seems tired and discouraged. You can't believe she was so brave to come out here alone.

But you know what Caroline is thinking—maybe brave, also foolish. All three of you could get enough demerits to completely ruin your playoff chances. And the summer's just begun.

"Do you want to walk back to camp with us?" you ask. "I think it's going to storm soon."

She quickly says yes.

Turn to the next page.

Over the next couple of days, you almost forget about the Cabin Cup. You go to Arts and Crafts with Caroline and learn about the wildflowers growing on Princess Island. You hike the island with Emerald, a Junior Counselor, and you both become quite skilled at recognizing plants.

Before bed one night, your Junior Counselor Pandora shows you and Caroline a book with a photo of Indian Pipe, the flower your cabin is named after.

"It's also called Ghost Plant," she says. "It's very rare, but it does grow on the island. Most plants and flowers make sugar out of sunlight using chlorophyll, but Indian Pipe is special. It gets energy from the trees, and it can grow in the dark. It usually grows by beech trees. At night, it glows."

You and Caroline grin but do not say anything. This is the flower you saw in the woods!

Go on to the next page.

But of course you can't tell Pandora about your nighttime adventure.

The next afternoon, you get a letter from your mother, Queen Helena. She and your father, King Edward, are on an official trip to Spain.

Turn to the next page.

Dear Peregrine,

I'm glad you're enjoying camp with Caroline. I met many friends there too as a girl! Mrs. Wiggins was one of my dearest friends. Perhaps she could tell you more about that missing Cabin Cup.

I've also written to your brother about it. Maybe you could solve the mystery together!

Much love,

Mom

P.S. Be kind to Cousin Millicent. XXOO

Go on to the next page.

Your mom has included a photo. It looks like her and Mrs. Wiggins when they were campers at Princess Island.

Turn to the next page.

You show the letter to Caroline. "We have to talk to Mrs. Wiggins!" you say. "She and my mom were campers here together when the golden Cup was stolen!"

"Are you actually going to write to Harold?" Caroline asks. "Could he really know anything? Would he help us even if he did?"

You wrinkle your nose. Harold is your brother, but he's not exactly your friend.

If you say, "I hate to ask Harold for help, but for once I need to," turn to page 44.

If you say, "I think getting Harold involved will just lead to trouble," turn to page 70.

"Is this what Bizzy was coming to see?" you wonder.

"I don't know, but it's time to get back," Caroline says.

There is no sign of Bizzy when you return to Indian Pipe. But she is there in her bed the next morning when the wake-up bells sound.

"How was your night?" you ask.

"I slept very well," Bizzy replies, smiling.

You never find out where she went. And you and Caroline never tell anyone about the strange magical scene in the mist.

The End

You decide to write to Harold about the missing Cabin Cup. The idea of working with him makes you ill. But he might have valuable information.

Besides, as your nanny Miss York always says, "you catch more flies with honey than you do with vinegar."

So you try to be as sweet as honey in your letter to your brother. You tell him you think he's super smart and he's the only one who can help on this very important search. You even offer to share credit with him if you find the missing Cup.

When you're done, you're exhausted. Being nice to Harold is tiring work.

Go on to the next page.

Letters go between the two islands every day on the Mail Boat. Harold writes you back just two days later, which is probably a record. You can tell it's from Harold because of the bad handwriting and spelling mistakes.

Dear Princes Dirt,

Your right, I'm smarter then you. So meet me at the beach tonight at 8 if its not raining. Be there on time or else!

Turn to the next page.

After dinner, while Millicent is at play practice, and Bizzy is at the barn braiding horses' tails for the horse trials tomorrow, you and Caroline sneak to the beach. All water sports are forbidden after dinner. Harold is waiting by his kayak, tapping his foot.

"It's 8:03, Princess Dirt," he says, holding up his wristwatch. "You are three minutes late."

"Whatever," you say. "What do you know about the Cabin Cup?"

That's when Harold pulls something out of his pocket. It's a map!

Turn to page 48.

You study Harold's map. There's an "X" by a big tree. And the word BEECH.

"I already checked out the beach," Harold says looking around. "But there aren't any trees here."

You roll your eyes.

You point to the word BEECH. "That's not the sandy kind of beach," you tell Harold. "It's a beech *tree*! There are lots of those on Princess Island."

Caroline adds, "The question is figuring out which one. There are too many to dig around them all. It would take three summers of camp."

You study the map again. You notice a tiny ghost hovering near the tree marked by an "X." You jump up and shout, "I've got it!"

"I need my shovel," you announce. "It's at Indian Pipe. Let's take the secret trail. That way no one will see Harold."

Turn to page 68.

You go back to the cabin and sneak into bed quietly. You wake up and it's still dark out, but you can tell hours have passed. Bizzy isn't back.

Her bed hasn't been slept in.

You nudge Caroline awake. "Something happened to Bizzy!" you whisper. "Maybe she went to the burial ground?"

"And suffered an ill fate?" asks Caroline, popping upright.

"Exactly. We have to help her!"

If you decide to hike to the burial ground to look for Bizzy, turn to page 24.

If you wait until morning to tell your counselor Pandora what happened, turn to page 60.

"Go ahead and take the map. We don't need it!" you holler.

Harold turns and disappears into the woods.

"We already know where that cup is buried," you remind Caroline. You pull your shovel out of your camping gear and lead her toward the trail. "Come and follow me."

The woods seem less scary than they did the other night. But you feel nervous as you get closer to the fern grove.

"Where should we start digging?" you ask.

Caroline points to a moss-covered patch of earth. "Maybe there."

Your shovel goes in easily. Soon you've dug little holes all around the log. You spot something shiny in the dirt, but it's way too small to be the Cabin Cup. You reach down and pull out an old silver locket.

Turn to the next page.

You wipe the locket clean and carefully open it. It contains two tiny photos—one of a handsome young man with a strong jaw and the other a woman with her hair in a fancy updo.

"It must be Lady Violet," says Caroline. "And this must be Mathew, the man she wanted to marry! It's so sad that her father kept them apart."

Turn to page 65.

"I think she's crying wolf," you say. "Millicent tricked us once already tonight. Let's not fall for it twice."

You make it back to the cabin, but Millicent doesn't—not for a long time. Finally, the door opens slowly. Someone stands in the doorway, crying and dripping wet. Is this the ghost? Bizzy flicks on the light.

It's Millicent, and her dress and hair are soaked.

"The g-ghost chased me," she sobs. "I g-got lost in the woods. It s-started to rain!"

You glance at Caroline. Now you feel terrible. She was telling the truth about the ghost!

"Here, dry yourself off, and get into your bunk to get warm," Caroline says, holding out a fresh towel.

Turn to the next page.

The three of you help Millicent out of her wet things and into some dry pajamas.

"The ghost was terrifying," she whimpers.

"You were brave and lucky, Millicent," you add, trying to be nice.

The next morning, your cousin wakes up with poison ivy all over. She has to scratch like crazy.

"Scratching is not princess-like," she moans.

You bring Millicent to see the camp nurse in the Main Lodge. When you tell the counselors what happened, you and Caroline get twenty demerit points each for sneaking around after dark—and forty more for leaving Millicent behind!

And to top it off? You never find out where the missing Cabin Cup is buried. You're certain Millicent knows something, but she's so mad at you that she clams up.

Now you may never know.

The End

"It *must* be Bizzy," you say. "Who else would be out here at night? Maybe something is wrong."

The words are barely out of your mouth when your boat strikes something hard.

"Oh no! We've hit a rock!" Caroline cries.

Suddenly your feet are wet.

"It made a hole in the hull. We need to bail!" you shout. You stand up looking around for something to use.

You find two small plastic cups, but they're not much help. The rowboat starts to sink.

"Grab on to this!" a voice commands.

"Bizzy!" you cry, just as you and Caroline are swamped. Your life vest keeps you afloat, but the lake is so cold, you can barely breathe.

"Grab my stern. I'll paddle you to shore," Bizzy commands.

You and Caroline have no choice. You grab the rear of the canoe.

Turn to page 18.

You turn around and run for it. You hear an eerie howling that gets louder and louder. It seems to be coming from a glacial boulder edged in thick vines.

Then you spot a bright green skirt swishing from behind the rock. This is no ghost—it's Millicent, playing a prank!

"Millicent! You come out from behind that tree right now!"

When she steps into view, you're furious.

"What's wrong with you? Why would you scare us like that?"

You don't wait for an answer. "Come on," you say, as you grab Caroline's hand and push past Millicent. You are determined to leave your pest of a cousin behind.

Turn to the next page.

You and Caroline are a ways down the path, leaving Millicent in the dust. Suddenly, you hear a piercing scream.

"Come back! Perri! Caroline! Help ME! She's come back! I'M TRAPPED!"

You and Caroline lock eyes. "Is she telling the truth?" whispers your friend, tightening her grip on your hand.

"I'm not sure. It could be just another trick," you say.

If you decide to go back to answer Millicent's cries for help, turn to page 29.

If you decide to ignore Millicent and keep walking, because that will teach her a lesson, turn to page 53.

At breakfast, you tell your Junior Counselor, Pandora, that Bizzy is missing. "She took a canoe out last night. After lights out. We think she was headed to the burial ground to meet someone," you say.

"How do you know?" Pandora asks.

You and Caroline exchange a look.

"We followed her," you admit.

"Well, I wish you had told me this last night," Pandora says gently. "I'll have to give you both twenty demerits. But thank you for telling me now." She hurries off to let the other counselors know.

Turn to page 67.

"I'm faster than you, Claptrap!" you yell.

You tear off straight into the bushes after your brother.

Harold has gotten faster and gets ahead. You lose him until he pops out of the woods at the archery center. Then he turns on a burst of speed and ducks into the stables.

Turn to page 63.

Horses whinny and stomp as you dash after him. You tiptoe toward an empty stall. *Ouch!* You crash right into Harold, who falls backward and into a steaming pile of fresh manure!

"Give me the map!" you holler. But Harold drops it into a pile of horse dung.

"It's all yours," says Harold. "Princess Poop!"

Harold hears a counselor approaching, jumps up, and runs away. Caroline runs up behind you out of breath.

"Where's Harold? Where's the map?" she asks.

You point to it, holding your nose.

"My nanny says never be afraid of a little dirt." With that she carefully plucks the map out of the manure.

"We'll wash this off, and it will be as good as new," Caroline announces happily. "Harold is a ninny. We'll find that gold Cabin Cup yet."

The End

You nod. "I know. She died of a broken heart. It can actually happen."

"You can also get scared to death," Caroline adds, as an owl *whoo-whooos*. As you study the locket, you feel a sudden cool breeze on your back.

An *eerie* white figure in an old-fashioned dress reaches for your hand.

"Is that mine?" she asks, her voice rising.

"I—I think so," you stammer. You set the locket on the log.

Lady Violet snatches it and opens it up. "Ah, Mathew," she sighs. "I've been looking for this for almost a hundred years."

But then she catches you watching, and whirls around. "I'll wait for a thousand years if I have to. Mathew promised me he would come back, and one day, wherever he is, I know he will."

Turn to page 86.

Word gets out that Bizzy has taken off and cannot be found. Rumors spread like wild fire.

"I think she was kidnapped," one girl says, spooning oatmeal into her bowl at the next table.

"No, she was meeting a boy from Prince Island," another states confidently.

The truth turns out to be much less exciting. Bizzy was caught in a current and carried five miles down the lake. She spent a very cold and uncomfortable night at the bird sanctuary.

"Not to mention that she ruined her dress by sleeping in bird poop," sniffs Millicent. "And she ruined our chances to win the Cabin Cup."

It looks like you are going to have to return to Princess Island another summer!

The End

You run to the end of the beach and walk a few feet into the woods. There it is! It's a trail you and Bizzy started last year when you had horseback right after sailing. As you run along, Harold grumbles from the rear. Boy is he slow! And whiney! "How far is it? I agreed to help find a trophy. Not start practicing for the marathon."

You stop at your cabin for your shovel. It was a special present from your father, designed for mountaineers. It's light but very strong.

When you reach the cluster of Indian Pipe flowers, you start to explain, "These are Ghost Plants. They're very rare, almost extinct. They aren't every place on the island. And this tree with the silvery bark is a beech tree. So the ghost on the map, next to the beech tree, might actually be these flowers!"

You dig near the Ghost Plants. When your shovel strikes something hard, your heart races.

Turn to page 8.

You shake your head. "Even if Harold knew where the Cabin Cup was buried, he'd never tell me. Let's go find Mrs. Wiggins."

You and Caroline link arms and head to the Main Lodge. You pass three nervous first-year campers, still wearing life jackets. Once they pass their swim test, they'll be able to go without them. You also pass Sam on her way to the horse barn. She is a horse nut. You and Caroline give her a jolly wave.

Finally, you find Mrs. Wiggins. She is enjoying a fresh pot of tea in the empty dining hall.

"Two of my favorite second-year campers!" she says, looking up. "How can I help you, Princesses?"

"My mom sent me this photo!" you tell her excitedly. "I wanted to ask you about it." Mrs. Wiggins takes the photo from your outstretched hand.

Go on to the next page.

"Oh, Queen Helena," she says, smiling. "Your mother was one of my best friends here on Princess Island."

Before you can ask about the Cabin Cup, Mrs. Wiggins raises a finger to her lips. "I have something for you girls, but it's top secret. Follow me."

Turn to the next page.

Mrs. Wiggins leads you down the path toward the cabins. When you reach Bunchberry, she examines the wooden boards just below the windowsill. "Let's see, it was here somewhere," she murmurs. When she pushes on a board, the other end lifts. "Oh, there it is!"

She slides out a folded piece of paper. It's water-stained and yellow with age. "This map is a clue," says Mrs. Wiggins, unfolding the paper. "The golden Cabin Cup was stolen while your mother and I were campers here, but we found this map left by the thieves. We hid it here in the window of Bunchberry, but we never found the Cup."

Turn to page 75.

You hold your breath as you examine the hand-drawn map. In the middle of a maze of trails, you see an "X." Beside the "X" is a large tree. And above the "X," someone drew a ghost! *That must be why Sam thought the Cup was buried in the graveyard*, you think.

"Now promise me, girls, that you will not look for it at night," says Mrs. Wiggins. "And you will not break any other camp rules in your search for the missing Cup."

You and Caroline both nod. "We promise."

"Okay then. I wish you good luck—and a great adventure." Mrs. Wiggins hands you the map with a wink.

As you walk back to Indian Pipe, twigs crackle in the woods nearby.

Turn to page 77.

"Who's there?" Caroline calls.

You glimpse a familiar blue polo shirt in the bushes, just like the boys on Prince Island wear. Is it Harold spying on you? You charge into the bushes. But no one's there.

Whoever it was, it wasn't Harold.

Back at your cabin, you hide the map safely in your camp trunk. Then you and Caroline walk to dinner. Along the way, you tell her your latest idea. "Remember when we saw the ghost of Lady Violet Grimm last summer?" you ask.

"Yes. She was sitting on a log in the fern grove, crying over her long-lost love, Mathew. I'll never forget it!" Caroline replies.

You nod. "But that wasn't just a log, Caroline. It was a huge fallen tree branch. Maybe Lady Violet was giving us a clue. Maybe the tree is the one on the map!"

Turn page 79.

After dinner, you hurry back to the cabin for the map. But as you step into your cabin, something is very wrong. Everyone's blankets are thrown around. Even Millicent is neater than this! Your trunk is wide open. And so is the window next to it. You race to the window and spot two blue polo shirts dashing into the woods.

"Hey!" you yell. "Stop!" You rush out the door after them. Up ahead you hear a branch break. Someone yells out in pain.

A few seconds later you come upon Harold and his best friend Andrew, the Duke of Crosby. Harold and Andrew are both lying on the ground. Andrew is holding his knee and moaning. Harold is holding your map in his clenched fist.

Turn to the next page.

"Give it back!" you shout. "That map is ours!"

Harold shakes his head. "No way! Mom wrote me a letter about this map! It's just as much mine as it is yours, Princess Dirt."

You cringe at the nickname. "Oh yeah, Prince Claptrap?"

It's Harold's turn to get mad. His face turns dark red. Suddenly he turns around and takes off, leaving his injured friend behind! Andrew gets up slowly and runs after Harold, despite his bleeding leg.

If you can remember enough of the map, let Harold go and turn to page 51.

If you decide to chase Harold to get the map, turn to page 61.

"The rocks below Witch's Hat," Bizzy replies. "Why were you following me?"

"It's more like what are you doing here?" you say. "Out alone! At night! In a canoe!"

You notice she does not answer your question.

"Come on," Bizzy says. "I'll canoe you back."

The next day, you have to tell your Junior Counselor Pandora what happened to the rowboat. Mrs. Wiggins herself demands to see the three of you.

"Girls, you are guilty of breaking multiple Princess Island rules. Those rules are in place for your safety. Each of you get 150 demerit points."

150 demerits! It might be a Princess Island record.

Your heart sinks as the demerits are announced at breakfast.

Turn to the next page.

"Wait! Shouldn't Bizzy get points for saving Perri and Caroline's lives?!" Millicent asks Mrs. Wiggins, standing up in front of the entire dining hall. A silence falls.

Mrs. Wiggins considers.

"You're right, Millicent," she says. "150 merit points to Bizzy for her braveness and her quick action. And twenty-five for you, Millicent, for sticking up for someone else." Maybe you aren't out of the running for this year's Cabin Cup after all!

The End

The three of you burst into Indian Pipe and slam the door shut behind you.

"What's going on?" Bizzy cries, sitting straight up in bed.

"It's a long story," you say. "But everything's okay."

"No thanks to me," says Millicent, her lip trembling. "I'm sorry I scared you and Caroline. It's just that you two do everything together! I was feeling so…left out."

Turn to page 12.

You and Caroline slowly step away. You feel sorry for Lady Violet. When you are far enough away, you and Caroline turn and run for it.

Back at the cabin, Bizzy stirs in her bed. Millicent is mumbling something in her sleep about a tea party.

As quietly as you can, you both slip into your bunks.

"Caroline?" you whisper.

"Yes?" she replies.

"It's too bad we don't get merit points for doing a kindness for a ghost!" you say stifling a laugh.

"Yes, but it still wouldn't make up for the merit points for finding the Cabin Cup," Caroline replies. "I am certain that finding the gold Cabin Cup is worth at least a thousand merits."

"You're probably right. But don't worry," you say. "We can try again in the morning. Goodnight."

The End

ABOUT THE AUTHOR

Shannon Gilligan began writing fiction for a living after graduating from Williams College in 1981. She has written over fifteen books for children, including eleven in the *Choose Your Own Adventure* series. Her work has been translated into more than twenty languages. She spent a decade working on story-based computer games in the 1990s. Gilligan's day job is publisher of Chooseco. She lives in Warren, Vermont but travels widely. She recently took up surfing.